SMOKE STACK
BLUES

A Book of Poems from
the Heart of the Unknown Writer

Written by:
James Ray Chaffin Sr.
a.k.a
The Unknown Writer

IBSN 13: 978-1533086105
IBSN 10: 1533086109

Contents

In Memorial of the Author

James Ray Chaffin Sr.

August 20th, 1956 – November 26th, 2012

Foreword

I am the authors son; James Ray Chaffin Jr.

My Father, James Ray Chaffin Sr., was born on August 20th, 1956 in rural Louisiana. He lived a life of simple means and remained unmarried until he met my Mother when he was 26. They soon got married and had me. The marriage did not work out, so when I was about 7 years old my parent's separated. It always takes two to tango so this book is not to reflect blame on one party or the other on the separation.

The separation that happened was hard on my father so he found an outlet and began writing the contents of this book of poems. He wrote during times of frustration, pain, and love. Often times he would be driving his 18 wheeler and think of a poem and pull to a safe place to park and begin writing. He found comfort in these poems and I hope you do too.

Getting these poems published was his lifelong dream so this is a tribute to his life and memory. I love you beaucoup Dad.

Family Quotes

These are a few words from James R. Chaffin Sr.'s parents (Gerald and Bobbie Chaffin).

"James was a loving son and always went out of his way to care for us. He lived out in his camper in our yard and we missed him when he was on the road. His Dad is in heaven now with Him and I (Mom) am happy with that. I love you my child; your Mom."

Bobbie Chaffin

"James Ray was a sweet and loving brother with a great gift that he left the world to enjoy for eternity. His passing left a hole in our hearts and family forever. With loving memory, your Sister,

Geraldine Mayo."

"James Ray Chaffin wrote this book of poems and he felt they were a reflection of his life and it is his way of sharing with us his heart, mind, and soul. Love always, your Brother,

David Chaffin."

"James Ray, your poems reflect on what kind of person you are; very thoughtful and loving. We miss and love you very much. Also you don't need to walk on your tip toes now you are as tall in heaven as you wanted to be here on earth. Love always, your Sister,

Brenda Lewis"

"I miss my Brother very much and wish he was still here with us but I am very happy he wrote and left behind these wonderful poems as his legacy. Your Brother,

Donald Chaffin."

"My brother James (weezie), was a light in my world. I love him very much. I am so glad that his son James Jr. is getting his Dads' book of poems out to the world. I know you people out there will enjoy the words of his life. Love you always, your Sister,

Sheryl Deville."

"My sweet brother, James Ray Chaffin Sr., was a prime example of (dynamite comes in small packages). He was a quiet and solitary person but when you were around him you couldn't ask for a more passionate and loving brother. The bible says that all your dreams would be full filled (maybe not on earth). I want to think he is sitting on a houseboat in heaven that he always dreamed of here on earth. I LOVE YOU BROTHER WITH ALL MY HEART AND MISS YOU. I"LL SEE AGAIN ONE DAY IN HEAVEN. Your loving Sister,

Christine Simmons."

"I am so proud of my Brother James Ray's accomplishment in writing this poetry. I miss being able to make him home made biscuits while he raided my refrigerator. I love and miss you dearly. Your Sister,

Rita Warren."

SMOKE STACK BLUES

It's nationwide, and country sides
I'm rolling down the road
That lonesome highway called my name
You know I had to go

It's wheels on the ground
With the pedal down, and
She's puffin that diesel smoke
This big old engine speaks to
Me every time she makes
 a stroke.

I gotta heavy load, with a
Rush up code, so I got no
Time to kill
So it's truck stop coffee, gotta
Keep on rockin' and feeling
That highway thrill

It's the highway blues that's
In my shoes, there's nothing
I can do
So I answered that call
I get through it all, and
Rock with the highway blues

I'll be jamming gears, stopping
For a beer, whenever I
Get the chance
There ain't nothing wrong with
A country song, and slow one
With a girl to dance.

LIFE

I've danced the dance of life
I've fought the duel of death
Life is but a score board
Do we fail or pass the test

Life's path, we all must travel
Though littered with sticks and stones
Which road should we take,
Which path is right or wrong

To waltz among the flowers
Or stroll into the woods
With mountains we must conquer
That we know we should

To stand upon that hill
Sword held up to the sky
Life's battle we must fight
Although we don't know why

A battle cry goes forth
I wage the war of life
To win it is a must
I'll change both day and night

DREAMS

I wish I had someone
Someone to love just me
Someone to share my life
To share my loving dreams

A person who will be honest
Someone who will be true
With a heart that really knows
How to love me too

With love that's sure to blossom
Bearing fruits of joy
A love that is so strong
No one could ever destroy

A person who loves by day
And holds me through the night
And, deep within her heart
I'm always in her sight

I've longed looked and searched
I've cried, wished and dreamed
My search goes on forever,
Forever is how it seems

HILL BILLY HEART

It's deep in the mountains
Where my heart was born
That the rivers and the hollows
Call without scorn

While I, a prisoner held
My spirit locked in time
Escape it is a must
Not only in my mind

To stand upon the mountain
And breathe its crystal breeze
I need the spirits touch
I need to fill their needs

To stand among the trees
And dart from rock to brush
To live upon the mountain
To me it is a must

The winds they call my name
I soon must fill the part
For deep inside this body
There is a hillbilly heart.

BABIES EYES

Now I wish
Upon a star
Please shine upon
That broken heart

But if you fit
To let me in
Please let me
Hold her once again

Guide her path
As on she goes
Through life's twisting
Winding roads

Please hear me now
This very night
And shine on her
With your loving light

And twinkling stars
That blinks the skies
Please dry the tears
From babies cries.

GOOD MORNING KATIE

Good morning Miss Katie
With your bright warm smile
That touches people's hearts
For thousands of miles

With eyes that are blue
You brighten our days
In so many charming
Sweet loving ways

Matt, I am certain
Is mesmerized
While blessed with your grace
And the twinkle in your eyes

Good Morning you say
With a sweet loving grin;
And; that's when I hit
The floor with my chin

Good Morning, I groan
From down on the floor
Then my little woman
Boots me out the door

Through the window I watch
Sneaking a glance
Catch me—she might
But it's well worth the chance.

MEMORIES OF MOTHER

I look upon my children
And think of times now past
Memories I hold so dear
That will forever last

I see them in the yard
As they play
The same as I once did
In my childhood days

I can almost hear it now,
Mothers beckon call
Her voice rang out with love
She loved us one and all

A meal prepared
That was a feast
Although at times
She wouldn't eat

And with old lard buckets
We'd kneel and pray
She'd thank the Lord
For each, and every day

Memories I hold so dear
It's her I so adore
I know she thought of me
When she walked through
Heavens doors.

ANGEL

She came to me
In graceful flight
With glorious colors
To lighten the night

Her hair is like
The summer breeze
That dances so gently
With all the leaves

Reflections of summer
Bloom from her hair
With golden rays
to enhance the air

She came to me
In graceful flight
Her love is so pure
So sweet and so bright

The wait I know
Was worth the pain
I lost the hurt,
An angel I've gained

JUDGE ME

One look at you
And my heart did flutter
I tried to speak
But started to stutter

A whisper from your lips
And my spirit ran free
Like an eagle it soared
Over mountains and trees

Your smile touched
The depths of my soul
In your beauty I lost
All self-control

Then ever so swiftly
You brought me down
Shot from the skies
I plunged to the ground

With words you cut
And pierced my heart
I saw your pain
And those broken parts

I felt the hurt
The unneeded abuse
For reasons unknown
There's no excuse

Please judge me well
But now me as one
Don't cast me aside
For what they have done

BLEEDING HEARTS

A heart gets broken
But someday will mend
It someone gently takes you
By the hand

With patience and time
With tender words so kind
You can mend this heart
One day at a time

No hurry no rush,
Will I ever be in
One second at a time
And, this heart just might mend

But scares will be there
Never to disappear
Cause when a heart gets
Broken, it usually tears

Stronger will it be,
Stronger than before
For now, to my heart
I've closed the door

I locked it up
Just as tight as can be,
For never again, will
This heart bleed.

THANKSGIVING DAY

To Christopher Columbus,
We now should bow.
He weathered the storms,
With winds that howled.

We must give thanks,
To our fore fathers.
And the children who lost,
Their loving mothers.

Our nations births,
We owe them all.
Their country needed.
They answered the call.

The fields, they charge,
that sang with lead.
Our freedom was played,
with blood they shed.

Our men and women,
They come to aid.
They'll give their life.
Our freedom they'll save.

With heads now bowed.
PLEASE! Let us pray.
To them we owe,
Our THANKSGIVING DAY!

LIFE GOES ON

To be a dad, is
Quite a chore
But, it is a job
I do adore

To change it now
Would be insane
For life no longer
Would be the same

An able body
We must be,
And stand by them
Through eternity

There's colds and flus
With doctor bills,
And sometimes fevers
That gives them chills

There's bumps and bruises
And skinned knees, and
May I have one Dad,
Oh, Can I please?

There's fishing, swimming
And camping out,
But there are those days
We could do without.

But then there's days
That are just right
Like; when they kiss the
Dog and the cat they bite

Then all too soon
They're grown and gone,
And there is
An empty room

Sometimes it seems
So hard to smile
But, wait; look, we
Have a grandchild!

SILENT CALL OF LOVE

Who are you people?
       it wasn't you that I called.
HEY, come back with that
       board, it's part of my wall.

Where is my family?
       the one with the kids,
That played in the snow
       and slid on the sleds.

HEY, that's part of my roof
       and the carpet it stays.
I'm certain they miss me,
       they'll come back someday.

Don't touch that window,
       they need it to see,
To watch those children
       while they play around me.

The porch it is his
       to sip coffee at dawn
While watching the birds,
       he'll stretch and then yawn.

Don't do this to them,
       bring back my doors,
Don't take down my walls
       or tear up my floors.

Come back with those faucets,
     my cabinets and lights
Cause-when they return,
     it could be at night.

I miss them so much.
     Why are they gone?
Why am I a house?
     When I once was a home!

ECHOES IN NIGHT

The whippoorwill sings
It's song of the night
As the wolf wails out
It's loneliest cry

He talks to the stars
And the man in the moon
For he knows his time
Is coming soon

He can feel the ground shake
And hear the roar
As the hunters on horses
Quickly close the door

Even now he knows
He'll take the fall
But this time he'll fight
With his back to the wall

He'll fight this battle
To the bitter end
And hope somehow, one of
Those bastards to hell he'll send

He's an old man now
And he's seen a lot
And knows damn well, it'll take
More than one shot

He charges in with the
Speed of light
You should have seen it,
Oh what a sight

The battle's on; and it's
a furious fight
He's giving it his best,
For it is his last night

They got him now
He breathes no more
But for two of the hunters
He closed their door

Lifeless he stands
In a trophy room
While folks gather around
To hear of his doom

But as a reminder
Of that gruesome fight
Old lightning bolts howls
They hear every night!

WANTED!

Wanted! Someone with whom
To share my life
A person who loves through
pain and strife

Someone with whom
To spend my days
A person who loves
In everyway

And when I have
Turned old and gray
They'll be with me
Throughout my days

And when life's book
Has reached the end
They'll hold me close
For my Amen

My heart it needs
That gentle touch
It needs true love
So very much

And add I'll run
Just like this
Wanted! Someone to
Love, to hold and kiss

SUN SHINE

Even in the darkness
That covers earth at night
We clearly see the beauty
Of your charming light

And early in the morn
Just before dawn
You chase away the gloom
To make us feel at home

You soothe us with a smile
Star glitter in your eyes
The truth of it shines
In you there are no lines

In time I know you wonder,
You've ask from time to time
Now there is no doubt
Why you're my sunshine

LOVING YEARS

Now to you
I give my life
My heart is yours
My darling wife

All through our life
Whether joy or tears
I'll stand by you
Throughout the years

When I'm at work
My heart still burns
To be with you
I do so yearn

I dream of you
When I'm asleep
It's in your arms
I am complete

We'll sound our trump
For all to hear
Our moment in time
Throughout the years.

A MOMENT IN TIME

I once walked through this world
With hardly no light
Not a smile had I seen
Could make it turn bright

But then in a second
In the blink of an eye
When I saw you walk in;
It was my moment in life

My heart was so heavy
Bounded down by the chains
The thunder did roll,
And it constantly rained
No change in the weather,
No relief in sight

But when you spoke
It was my moment in life

And when upon my hand
You did place a ring
The flowers did bloom
And the birds did sing

But when I heard those words,
Your now husband and wife
I knew in my heart
This was my moment in life

Never in a life time
Can our memoires be destroyed
For we have shared our laughter,
Our love and our joy

And together we have grown
Feeble and old
We know the love in our hearts
Will be young and bold

And then we'll thank the lord
For being so kind
For he let us together
Share a moment in time!

LOVING TREE

I throw no caution
To the wind
For a new relation
I will so begin

Loves seed I'll plant
And make it grow
I work the soil
Nice and slow

With gentle hands
And a loving touch
I'll water this seed
But not too much

Both day and night
It shall grow
I'll fill it need
My love will show

A beautiful thing
It shall be
For it will soon
Be a lover's tree

MY WORLD

I travel through time
From place to place
Back through the door
Of a now darkened space

I walk ever so slowly
Through each room
And see all of the joy
That ended to soon

I now see the ghost
Of laughter and fun
And wish that I
Could from it run

But another ghost
Has come into sight
As a reminder, of our
Once loving nights

I wish they would leave
And go far away
But here comes the ghost
From our wedding day

I close the doors
To keep them all out
But the room is still filled
With the words they did shout

I escape through a window
And through time I am hurled
To this dark empty place
That is now my world.

MY SON OF SEVEN YEARS

I have a son he's so much fun
And our names are all the same
And I love to watch this son of mine,
While playing those precious childhood games

In his school he makes me proud
He does so very well
When I look at his work, it starts
My heart with pride to swell

It's A's and B's, thank you, please,
Can I help you fix it, Dad?
And it really breaks my heart
To see him being sad

Upon his precious little face
Should never be a tear,
So I'll try to always bring a smile,
Upon the face of my son of Seven Years.

LOVE BY THE SCORE

No lonely nights
Or days of dread
I am alive,
No longer dead

Sunny days and nights
With stars
Love and joy, now lives
In my heart

A future I have
Now in my grasp
My heart you have
Now unlatched

The test you passed
Without much task
So much you have given,
So little you have asked

A secret passage I hid
From all
The key you found
And with love did call

No sharing my heart,
My feelings I horde.
But now it's yours
With love by the score.

THE STORM

The storm is here its winds are
Mighty, it boils within the soul
Its anger has reach new levels
The heart is solidly freezing

It brings pain and strife striping
The laughter it soon does kill
The heart is dead it beats no more
And soon beings to chill

The eyes did so clearly show
The light of life did shine
The life is gone; they'll shine no more
Through the endless times.

SEARCH OF LOVE

Why do we in life
So desperately search
For the one true love
That will us never hurt

Is there truly a love
That honest and meek
Could our hearts be doomed
Forever to seek

How does it begin
When does it start
How does so simply
Consume the heart

The eyes they will glow
The reflections of fire
Burning with need
of that yearning desire

A touch of the hand
With a passionate kiss
And when they are apart
Each other is missed

Myself I find
An answer I need
Is love worth to chance
A heart left to bleed

THE MOUSE

It was so quiet
That adorable little mouse
As it scurried about, all
Through the house

The cat she bolted,
But much too late
She sniffed about,
She now patiently waits

Out you go, you
Vicious cat
I do mean business,
And that is that

I see it run
I watch it play
I love to watch it
Throughout the day

It chews on this
And gnaws on that
Now where the hell
Is that sorry damn cat

Oh yea I know
A trap I'll set
I'll get that critter
I get him yet

I've set a dozen
Or maybe more
Still he chews the wood
On all the doors

I got you Cat
Now in you go
In the window I peek
To watch the show

He threw us out
Just the other day
He took my house
Away

Look! - Can you see
It; laughing at the cat
And me

Now from my tent
The cat and I
We sit and watch
We sob and cry

PERFECT ME

To look upon the mirror
It is so easy to me
The reflection, it is so perfect
Because it is of me

In me perfection lives
It shows beyond compare
My eyes, my smile, my body,
And even in my hair

If I smile and wink
I'll let you sign the list
But don't approach me ever
Unless you I've blown a kiss

Please restrain yourself,
If I speak to you
I need my space to breath,
Don't stick to me like glue

To look upon the mirror,
Is so easy for me
My reflection has been perfected
So perfect for all to see!

LAYED TO REST

My heart it died
Sometime ago
It was so young
But now its old

It lingered on
Too scared to dream
It needed love
And a song to sing

To be fulfilled
Was the need
It ached so bad
With tears to bleed

A thousand drops,
A million or more
It lost the love
It so adored

The smell of death
Now lingers near
I begged and pleaded
You would not hear

This heart I have
Now laid to rest
There is no hope
No more no less

My heart is dead
It is long gone
The grave is soon
To be its home.

DISTANT DEBATE

Here in the silence
Of a distant debate
I listen to the sounds
While it grows so late

I now live
In the present past
And relive the pain
That will always last

Of love, need,
Anger and hate
What I must do
I now debate

Escape from it
I cannot find
For always it must live
Deep in my mind

I must answer the call
And fill the need
I may lose
But I will succeed.

TO HAVE KNOWN SHERRON

Thanks girl for
The time we've spent
Although an illusion
It was heaven sent

My heart did glow
And burn for a while
With a bright new outlook
And a face that smiled

The rays of light
Did flow with ease
As they made their way
To the eyes in need

Now don't be sad
Or feel all alone
For it had been a delight
To have known, a lovely lady,
Known as Sherron

STARTING OVER

A change I have
Made for me
A different man
I will be

My life is now
In my grasp
I can no longer
See in the past

I've burned all bridges
There are no ties
I watch the flames
A bid them goodbye

A few things I now
Have in my heart
A new life, a new me
And now a new start.

FOREVER NO DREAMS

To wait and say
It will be soon
It would have meant
I was a fool

High hopes I held
That you would show
I figured a lie
So now I go

It now lays
Upon the ground
As though it were lost
And can't be found

A never ever
Circle of life
Of constant heart ache
Pain and strife

Like shattered glass
So are the dreams
Just like the hopes
Of this golden ring

LOST NOT FORGOTTEN

I drift and drift
To a place unknown
To a strange surrounding
That to me has never been shown

Trees with no leaves
Grass that is brown
Roads that are dark
And holes in the ground

Farther I drift, to
A drab sort of house
Where evil surrounds, and
It's quiet as a mouse

One window does glow
With an innocent light
And I drift closer, to behold
A beautiful sight

Surroundings to me
That are unknown
But the light that does shine
Comes, from my little son.

IF DREAMS CAME TRUE

What would you do
If dreams came true
Would you really know
The dream is for you

When passion ignites
With love it explodes
With earth shuttering tremors
Like volcanoes explode

Sparks soon to rise
To heaven they'll fly
To lighten the dark
Like stars in the sky

When love gently flows
Like lava down hill
Covering our hearts
So they can be healed

If dreams came true
Of love and of life,
With our day complete
As well as the nights.

If Dreams Came True!

WINTER'S KISS

The land now kissed
With winters frost
While naked trees
By the winds are tossed

The sun will peak
Above the trees
That have been striped
Of all their leaves

Ice and snow
And rain will fall
As old man winter
Comes to call

Creeks will rise
And sing with rage
Melodies to the forest
Like notes on a page

Creatures of wild
Will roam the land
While old man winter
Will deal his hand

The season's our fourth
Still yet the first
A year will die
To another one's birth.

HARVEST MOON

Someday this body
Will no longer morn
And it won't feel the pain
From a heart that is torn

It may be the day, when through
This body the cold wind has blown
When the eyes become set
And the heart is like stone

When life itself
This body does part
And nerves can no longer
Speak to the heart

No more will the arms
The fingers command
No longer will her body feel
The tenderness of the hands

The lips will no more
Search for the kiss
And love will the soul
No longer miss

The day is coming
And it may be so
For I can now see the fullness
Of a bright harvest moon.

UNDEFEATED

My mind is tired
My body grows weak
But I will not
Admit defeat

This war I've fought
For months and months
And I've yet to see,
A battle I've won

My body aches
From my head to my feet
But I will not
Admit defeat

My back is now
Against the wall
My legs they threatened,
To let me fall

I am surrounded
There's no escape for me
But never shall I
Admit defeat.

LAUGHTER FROM WITHIN

Laughing from within the heart
I think this is where
The healing really
Gets its start

Life being full of
Fun and joy
And the heart starts
To mend from being destroyed

I told you that
Time would tell
But if you don't watch it
You could again, fall under its spell

Little things, like
A home and a wife
And the feelings of
Living come back to life

The blood once again
Starts to pump
And your heart now
Begins to steadily thump

Once again your
Hearts on fire
Because it's for her
you have a burning fire

MURDER IN THE FIRST DEGREE

Oh what a sad life
It will have to be
To never again
Be truly free

My worst fears
Have come to life
And is all because
Of an unfaithful wife

Shouldn't she be charged
With first degree
For within my heart
She has murdered me

Try as I may but,
I just can't contend
With the feeling I feel
From deep within

Oh I feel love,
But just for a while
But in no time at all
I lose that smile

I called the doctor
And here what he said
It's bad news son
Cause your hearts dead

There isn't a thing
That I can do
Cause your hearts shattered
And totally bruised

So tell me your honor
Can you now see
Why the charge should be
Murder in the first degree?

FEEL THE PAIN OF BITTERSWEET

Read these words
And feel the pain
How it comes in waves
Like the pouring rain

It floods the heart
And drown the soul
And upon the body
It takes its toll

It never lets up
But steadily gains
Like the furious winds
of a hurricane

It picks up strength
Quickly gaining speed
Destroying everything
And doing as it pleases

Here taste it now
The bittersweet
Can you understand
Why revenge is a need

Don't worry now
Not one thing will I do
Cause God has assured
Yours—is coming soon

HARD FEELINGS

Now once again
I pace the floor
Wondering when I'll
Again walk through that door

Am I a prisoner
Forever to stay
Will I again
Be free

Bring locked up
To me is wrong
I'm charged with something
I haven't done

Now let me tell you
About a witch
She's like a mama
She's a whore and a bitch

Now you may know
She cut me deep
But I will not
Be the last to bleed

And when all of this
Is said and done
I know for sure
I will have won!

REMEMBER ME

When you strike a match
To light the flame
Think of your friend
Please say my name

And while the fire
Leaps to the stars
I'm there will you
Deep in my heart

Please give a speech
Of our times passed
A toast to me
Is what I ask

Upon that hill
were cheerful days
I cherish them all
In every way

And to the ladies
It's in good cheer
While sipping wine
Or drinking beer

Southeast I am
Oh what a pity
So—please boldly stand
And flash them tities

HEART OF STONE

Down that path
We did stroll
Hand in hand
To lover's cove

Around the curves
And up some hills
And not one drop
Of love did we spill

But then, one dark
December night
While looking upon
Those Christmas lights

The road so suddenly
Made a split
And your hand from
Mine seem to slip

What you did see
Looked so grand
But it was painted
By an evil hand

Now all your friends
Are long gone
And you have been
Left all alone

For each bridge you did
So eagerly burn,
And now to late
You have learned

Not one single bridge
Can you repair
For I will not with you
My heart share

And while through years of tears
And eternal grief
While in search of love
And sweet relief.

THE LAST STOP

I first saw her
At the truck stop Tiger
And as I talked to her, my
Blood pressure climbed higher and higher

She said her name
Is Connie Lynn
And I know I could love
Her from deep within

I wish some way
I stood a chance
And I sure would like
With her to dance

She has a man
And his name is Parrish
And her love he does
So much cherish

Now comes a day
I do so dread
And that's the day
They are to be wed

And from my heart
I do so much
Wish these two
The best of luck

BY YOUR HAND

There lies a waste
Upon our land
A creation of darkness
Made by your hand

Land now charred,
Dark and cold
No love, no light,
No heart of gold

Fields of green,
And water once cool
Now are deserts, and
Dried up pools

Trees now barren
Lies on this land
Deprived of life
By your hand

A hole now lies
Between our hearts
My trust you broke
And drove us apart

Replant, the seed of
Life if you must
But, it will not grow
In this desert dust.

DECREE

A decision is made
She has decreed
I must die
And slowly bleed

I wish to live
To hope and dream
All hope for me
Is gone it seems

A taunted talent
Imprisons my mind
Again I'll die
One last time

My heart I gave
To her in trust
But now I find
It has been crushed

Tonight I'll die
I'm dead indeed
I must die
She has decreed.

THE LOST HEART

The coyotes howled
All through the night
I could clearly hear
From my camp site

The crickets and locust
Serenade to me
They sing so sweetly
For me to sleep

When I awake
I stretch and yawn
While sipping my coffee
I watch the dawn

The birds they sing
To welcome the light
Preferring the day
Over the night

Squirrels they chatter
Going, from tree to tree
Enjoying the food
God gave 'em to eat

Again, I stalk the trails
And forge the cracks
While hunting for food
So I might eat

A house a home
I need again
I lost it all
Because she sinned

I bare the pain
I've paid the cost
My heart my son
It's all been lost.

WHO PLANTED THE SEED?

When all my troubles
Came along and
Everything in life
Did go wrong.

I asked the Lord, why me?
He gently answered,
You planted the seed.

Now I did tell you,
Long ago
You shall reap
Whatever you sow.

And you did plant those
Sinful seeds, but now
They've grown into
Ugly trees.

But now that you've
Come to me and ask,
I'll chop them down
With my mercy ax.

Now when life's storms
Come your way, just
Come to me and humbly
Pray.

For I'll calm the waters and
Still the winds and give you
Peace from deep
Within.

THE GOLDEN STONE

It's happening again, the poetry
Within, and like a river it does flow
It all comes from one little place
And sometimes sounds like a song

The heart is where it all begins
And there it does grow
And now I listen to my heart
I know it'll do me wrong

Although to others it may seem
My heart is icy cold
But when it speaks, it speaks
To me with words laced in gold

BIRTHDAY

I know it is your birthday
And the wish belongs to you
But if I could wish upon it
I know just what I'd do

I wish upon the candles
And pray to God above
I'd thank him most of all
You choose me to love!

MRS TONY

Everybody stops
At the 141
They know they'll
Have lots of fun

It's just off of
Interstate twenty
Where the coffee's hot
And the food is plenty

It is a place
That's well known
And they always make
You feel at home

We all know it
As the Bee Bayou
That's where I go
When I get the blues

It is so peaceful
And very homey
When the waitress
Is Ursula Tony

So ya'll come by
And see Miss Tony
And tell her to cut the bull—
And keep the bologna!

BLIND ILLUSIONS OF LOVE

How can they say
That love is free
Or believe that happiness
Will forever be

Cause when love dies
Only then can you see
That now, love has planted
A hatred seed

But for your heart
It's too late, it's colored in blue
For loves great illusions
Has hidden the truth

Look in the past
And see all the signs
Now you know, that
Love is truly blind

GHOSTLY MEMORIES

Who has seen a ghost
Neither you or I
But, I have heard
Their haunting cries

It's a piercing scream,
That cannot be heard
Although it is of
A thousand words

The echoes are silent
From a love that is dead
No sound can be heard
Except in my head

In time you will heal
That's what I am told
Yet the pain still grows
Deep in my soul

You must move forward
Don't live in the past
But their ghostly memories
Seem to last and last

If only their ghost
Would leave me alone
I'm sure I could
Build a new home.

TOUCH ME NOT

Watch it heart, don't
Let them in
You're still in danger
While trying to mend

She's already made it,
She's already in
Damn you old heart
What a fool you've been

Better pull back now
Someway, somehow
She could tear you apart
Even right now

The pain was tough
The bleeding too much
How could you allow
Yourself to be touched

Can you honestly say
Without a shadow of a doubt
You're ready for that touch,
The hurting's all out

You came out all broken
So give it some room
Right now you're not ready.
Why try so soon?

THE DAWN

Redbirds chirping, blue birds singing
House wren welcomes the light
While they were sleeping, a
Whippoorwill sang in the night

Raccoons chattered, a fox did bark
Beavers worked till dawn
Before the sun lit the sky
A doe gave birth to a fawn

Turtles paddle through the water
Looking for bait to steal
My bait it finds with a hook
And gets a mouth full of steel

Chicken hawks squawk, Roosters Crow
It time to rise and shine
An old catfish swims about
It's food it hopes to find

Rabbits hop into the night
Nibbling grass and seeds
At dawn when I awake I know
God gave us all we need!

STRONG BLOOD

I lost all hope
But still held on
It was the tears
That make me strong

I cried the tears
Of certain death
Somehow I lived
To face the test

Upon the stars
I danced the dance
I lived for love
I took a chance

Tears I've cried
From broken parts
The color was red
That flowed from the heart

She held a weapon
But not of steel
It was my blood
She tried to kill

I walk with pride
I thought was gone
The tears of blood
They made me strong.

DELETE!

I climb the mountain of life
Look at my tattered feet
Then look into the future
Upon the living sea

Their waters lay deep and blue
With rolling hills that wave
Come lay your cares upon us
They call both night and day

Let cool winds blow upon
And sooth your weary mind
Your cares will be forgotten
They'll vanish with the tide

Reflection they will cast
Pictures of soothing light
Your spirit can sail upon us
Our breath will give you flight

Look down I do but once,
And rub my bleeding feet
They reach out to the ocean
But- someone they hit Delete!

I look up to the mountain
I cannot see the peak
I place one foot now forward
To find that living sea.

THE BEAST WITHIN

One hot August day
Our eyes chanced to meet
The flames of desire
Spoke of our needs

Her eyes, they were blue
Our hearts were entwined
Words never spoken
Told every line

Eyes held each other
With heart locked in time
With the instincts of an animal
We felt all the signs

In her I was lost
I felt like a ghost
In those precious moments
I felt more than most

I dare not approach
Fear gripped my heart
The beast that lived
Could be torn apart

HAVE I?

What have I done
Or accomplished today
Did I help someone
Somehow, someway

If I make millions
My writing be heard
If I sold every line
Every little word

Is what I've done
Truly worthwhile?
Did I at least today
Make somebody smile?

Will I be like others
Just watch them bleed
Or will I be a friend
When they are in need

Have I reached out
That helping hand
Have I been a friend
To my fellow man

A passing word of hope
And good cheer
Could help someone for a moment;
For a day; or even a year.

DANCE WITH YOU

Dance with me, my love
I now beg of thee
Your heart needs our touch
This much I can see

I armed with your smile
Eyes shining like stars
And an old leather hat
Littered with scars

Dance with me lady
I'm here for your heart
Now is the time, to
Repair broken parts

For years I have searched;
Traveling long and far
Your love; it was my light
It shinned from the stars

It pointed my way
Faithful and true
My princess I must
Dance with you.

HORSE OF STEEL

It takes a special
Type of breed
To control the power
And fill the need

He must know the strength
Within the beast
And oh how its
Power can be unleashed

With a puff of smoke
It greets the world
With eyes of glass
And two small doors

It is a beast
This horse of steel
With a shiny grill
And 18 wheels

A diesel engine
And 13 gears
And dual antenna's
That are it ears

It gives an awesome
Mighty roar
Then charges on
To do its chore.

PEACE UPON THE LAND

Why do our people cry?
Why do our mother's morn?
Why do our children die?
Even those that were unborn

When Hitler shed your blood
Our country came to aid
Our blood stained the ground
Their lives paved the way

Does now your country weep?
Does fear grip her heart?
Such grief you have brought
With violence you had to start

Smoke now stains your skies
While fear grips them all
The pain we all feel
Your domain, it must fall

To work out in the fields
With our fellow man
There should be no need for war
Let peace rule the land.

BLEEDING HEARTS

A heart gets broken
But, someday will mend
If someone gently takes you
By the hand

With patience and time
With tender words so kind
You can mend this heart
One day at a time

No hurry, no rush
Will I ever be in
One second at a time
And this old heart, just
Might mend

But scares will be there
Never to disappear
Cause when a heart gets broken
It usually tears

Stronger will I be
Stronger than before
For now, to my heart
I have closed the door

I locked it up, just
As tight as can be
For never again, will
This heart bleed.

WILDERNESS OF NEED

You're looking so hard
In earnest you seek
But, you can't see the forest
For all of the trees

Through every little meadow
And valley you weave
Not seeing the birds
Much less the trees

The sturdy old oak
Or long living pine
That weathers the storms
One day at a time

You look high and low
Turn each little stone
Your mission is love
You dream of a home

In earnest you seek
Love fills the need
But you cannot see the
Forest for all the trees

GREED

It may be what
I fear the most
It looks as though
We'll pay the cost

Selfish games they
Play for keeps
Though we're the ones
That will have to bleed

The gain for self
That is their goal
At the expense
Of a sweet loving soul

Deceitful greed, it's
Their demand
It matters not
They'll deal the hand

Oh what joy
To win the pot
Our hearts are broke
But it matters not

It'll take your heart
I'll watch it bleed
I don't care. Now give;
Give more to me

THE LIVING DEAD

Who wants a person that
lives for only a while
But in no time at all
He dies from inside

Or a person whose eyes
That will glitter and glow
Then all of a sudden
They're dead and cold

He lives for a moment
So free and wild
But in a split second
He can no longer smile

Love I say is like
Taking a test
Sometime you fail, although
You've done your best

You know a test
You can retake
But with a heart
It's much too late

Who wants this old boy
That's all broken and used
With a heart that's been
So well abused

Who wants a body
That has no life
With a heart that's dead
From a killer wife.

Who wants a man
That's empty and void
Tell me, who wants someone
That has no joy

I am just a shell that's barely alive,
I am now both, dead and alive.

I REMEMBER

I took a trip
Into the past
Where once lived a love
That could not last

That little trailer house
It's white and brown
And the steps I built
From the porch to the ground

They were still there
They're almost the same
But so much is different
Cause everything has changed

An innocent love
In me was born
My heart I gave
But it was torn

I remember now
That passion we shared
Still, I remember how,
You never cared.

GAMBLING WITH LOVE

Everyone knows that
Love is a gamble
And if you lose at loves game
It will leave your heart in
Shambles

Just when you think
The game you will win
You find out too late, somebody
Has cheated, somebody
Has sinned

You can build a house
Make it a home
Then suddenly find
Your left all alone

No longer inside
Lives any warmth
And all of the walls
Are ragged and worn

With hammer and nails
And boards from a tree
You build a home
Her heart will be pleased

With patience and time
With hard work and love
You showed loving feeling

While building new cabinets
And buying new rugs

Sometimes you win
When love is the bet
But if you lose
The penalty is death.

WRITTEN IN LEAD

Blood flying, heart crying
Tears stream down my face
I'm lost in this world
Like drifting through space

My heart has been pierced
Lies are her words
No truth will she tell
Her tongue is the sword

Come look through the pages
Read every line
Read how this man
Was stabbed with her lies

No gun, no bullets
Will ever be found
No prints did she leave
Not even on the ground

Words from my heart
Are written in lead
My heart; it passed on
It is now dead.

GOLDEN HEARTS

She had a heart
As pure as gold
Full of love, that would
Never grow old

A heart so kind
As sweet as could be
Until it was broken
And made to bleed

He stole that heart
Made of gold
Left her a heart
So dead and so cold

Her loved, he aged
At a high rate of speed
Until his love
No longer was a need

I'll heal that
Soul cast for doom
I must not forget
To give some room

The bleeding,
Lord if I may
Replace it with love
Forever to stay

That heart I'll take
So dead and so cold
And ever so gently
Turn it to gold.

JUST MISSING YOU

Missing you girl
Has been a breeze
Hugging you tight
Has become my need

Friends I say
That's all I ask
Lover no more
What a hell of a task

Friends I say
Is plenty for me
But your sweet loving
Is my greatest need

Your loving arms
To hold me tight
That's what I need
All through the night

TOGETHER AGAIN

It's Christmas morning
I look to the sky
With tear filled eyes
I silently cry

To the west I look
Where my son soon
Will awaken to presents
In that room

Another year
A day of dread
Again I'll weep
While in my bed

I wish to see him
On this day
It tears me apart
In so many ways

God help me please
I ask of thee
My child I miss
And desperately need

While Christmas cheer
Spreads over the land
Please touch him Lord
With thine on hand

And tell him please
I think of him
We'll be together
Someday again!

I THINK OF YOU

I think of you
Most everyday
Into the past I reach
In loving ways

Around the fires
Are memories to adore
You showed compassion
And so much more

With outstretched arms
you passed the test
I needed a friend
You are the best

The hill you shared
Words just can't say
It meant so much
In every way

This note I write
With love I say
You are the best
In everyway

CALL OF THE WILD

I long to be
Among the trees
Running bare footed
On a carpet of leaves

The call I feel of
Rivers and streams
The creatures of wild
Even the birds that sing

To stalk a prey, a
Squirrel or rabbit
I am a creature
Of a natural habit

To stretch a line
With a baited hook
And catch a fish
With that hungry look

It is my need
I must fulfill
With cool crisp nights
And dawns early, morning chill.

A FRIEND I SEEK

A friend is what
I really did need
Someone like you
I had so earnestly sought

But with a sudden
Jolting shock
We were lovers
My world you rocked

Passionate loving
My heart did need
You opened my heart
You found the key

You filled it up
With kisses and hugs
While we made love
On that magical rug

I had my friends
Even a home
But: without a mate
A man is alone

Someone with whom
To share his life
A man's best friend;
It is his wife.

IMAGE

An image of darkness
On the glass did appear
A shadow then darkened
Throughout the years

No hope for love
That's what appeared
The picture it was aged
Beyond its natural years

To look upon the mirror
It was so hard to do
But all has changed,
All because of you

You walked into my life
Just to lighten the way
You gave me back my life
Your life has saved the day

You are my loving heart
My sweet and loving Queen
You are so much more
You are my every dream

A WARM SUMMER FREEZE

A summer breeze dances with leaves
While flowers wave to the sun
A beautiful woman to try and please
With her it's so much fun

Nine years you share, sweet loving care
And then one day it's gone
She up, out and all about, and
Then she's up and gone

Heart is broken; it torn apart
It longer will be strong
For now, it has been damaged
By a killer summer storm

Now you see the falling leaves
Winter will soon be here
Dying words that should be heard
No one will ever hear

It's ice and snow, all is frozen
With no summer sun to heat
It won't be long until
The heart cannot beat

Words untold come out of the soul
From all those wasted years
But I must keep going on
For my son of seven years.

HOLE IN MY CHEST

Where did it go
Why has it left
Why is there now
A whole in my chest

Now this house
All hollow and chard
Signs that I read
There written in the stars

Darkness with tears
A face with a frown
No laughter is there
Just dark empty sounds

No light or no joy
Silent invades
The body's engulfed
With heart rendering days

I know I must seal
This hole in my chest
Patch it I must
And take back the rest

UNTIL

Until you've been
Inside of a man
Or walked in his shoes
That leave his prints
Upon the sand

Until you've lived
His painful rage
That writes upon
His hearts page

Until you've seen it
Through his eyes
Things that deceive
With hurting lies

Until you've lived
Inside that man
You never know, why
His heart is hard or
Where he stands

Until you've seen
Those calloused hands
You'll never know- until
You've been inside a man.

A WINNERS PAIN

The battles of battles
Has started this night
And she hasn't a clue
I've started to fight

Slipping through trees
As quite as a mouse
Without so much as a peep
While approaching the house

Darting eyes, they search
And they seek
Observing the foe
While their fast asleep

Giving the signal
With the blink of an eye
The enemy is now
Caught by surprise

It may last as hour
A day or a year
With the smell of victory
And the end very near

So many battles she's
Won from the start
Not caring if she started
A war in my heart

Although this war
I will have won
I'll still feel the pain
Of my little son.

JUST ME AND YOU

When I look into
Those eyes of blue
It brightens things up
For a day or two

And when her face
Lightens up with a smile
It cheers me up
For miles and miles

This girl you know
I do adore
As I watch her walk
Across the floor

I wonder if this
Lady from Epps
Knows how I've
Yearned to kiss her lips

Or how these hands
That are so calloused
Need to gently touch
This girl from Dallas

It matters not
Her family tree
All I want, is
This woman to please.

MY LADY

Her honor I now
Must embrace
With the blood that now
Through my veins race

My life is hers
I must answer her call
She is my lady,
My Queen, my all

My anger it is
As blackened steel
Forged in the fire
Tuned in the reel

A monster he is
Thou deemed a Knight
Soon I will strike
With all my might

Upon his chambers
Stony floors
I'll shed his blood
And mark the doors

I took the oath
I will uphold
To her I give
My heart and soul

BROTHERLY LOVE?

Am I to you
Somehow kin
Were we ever
Truly friends

I know our blood
It is the same
And we do both have
The family name

We have the same father
As well as mother
But deep in my heart
We're no longer brothers

Lying awake
Sometimes I cry
Wishing I could
Completely die

Forgiveness you've ask
For what you've done
But now I must ask
Where is my son?

Inside my heart
There is no joy
For; I no longer have
My little boy

Enjoy your family
Everyday
Just remember; you
Help take mine away

POISONED LOVE

Like the water that flows
From a clear mountain stream
So pure, so sweet
And totally clean

It constantly flows
Until a river it meets
Like the love for my wife,
That once lived in me

It starts so small
But constantly flows
Until in one big mass
It steadily grows

Sometimes from the sun
It glitters with sparks
Like the pure sweet love
That lived in my heart

But now that stream has ceased to run
And the water is stale
Like that of a pond

The river has stopped
It's grand finale
All that is left
Is a dried up old valley

And like toxic waste

To a river will stain
So have you poisoned,
The blood in my veins

IT TAKES MORE

A day in the woods
On the mountain in spring
Just me and my lover
And a river that sings

To talk by the waters
While rapids do roar
She's ever so gentle
Unlock my hearts door

A roll in the hay
That's not how it's done
It's talking and laughing
And all sorts of fun

While raking and cleaning
Loving and more
Together it's done
Two; must open the door

All of the keys,
They can be found
But open them gently
Make every move count!

FRIENDS?

Can you not see
The look in his eyes
That deep in his heart
He constantly cries!

Friends in the distance
They cannot hear
Although they appear
So incredibly near

Somewhere from afar
Came a horrible scream
They know from the feeling
It's a heart killing scene

Somewhere in the distance
Some agonizing cry
It tells them so clearly
the heart soon will die

I'd help you my friend
If only I could
Words from their hearts;
Hearts made of wood

They'll be here for me
Through all of my time
With their hand out stretched,
For a dollar or a dime.

LEFT FOR DEAD

My heart was pierced
I was left for dead
She wished me death
But I lived instead

Lay to rest?
In her tortured dreams
She holds no love for life
Is how it seems

I live my life
I shared my dreams,
Of love, of life, and the
Beauty it brings

To share but one;
One word of passion
How we need each other
And love ever lasting

Left for dead
Her fantasy it seems
I am alive, with
Sweet loving dreams

MOVING ON

We waited for you
All that we can
Our little boy
Will soon be a man

A tower I built
Constructed of my heart
For years I keep watch
We held up our part

You said you were bored
Then you were gone
No regard did it hold
For him or our home

We needed we hoped
Held open the door
But now I must say
We're now getting bored

Wait! That we did
All that we can
There's no more waiting
Inside of this man

THE INNOCENT LOSERS

The battle has started, the
Fighting has now begun
Now when this war has ended
Let's see who's really won

Although a winner you may be
In time you will see
That in a war of any kind
Nobody has really won

The one who suffers
Most of all, will be
The little ones
For they will pay the
Ultimate price, for
The wrong they haven't done

What can I say, or even do,
To take this pain away,
I'll hug them each
One by one, through
Their childhood days.

KEEPER OF THE DOOR

Welcome back
You long lost friend
The door that died
Now lives again

A door of steel
That held me down
Has now been crushed
Into the ground

A thing of beauty
Came by to chance
She gave me life
So I might dance

Thoughts now fade
Of how it sealed
All covered in rust
And well concealed

The key is your
Forever more
You are the keeper
Of the door

TWO HEARTS

Two hearts that live
And beat as one
Can only beat
When they are joined

In hoped and dreams
In love they thrive
So vibrantly they beat
They are alive

Apart they hurt
And share the pain
They beat together
They are the same

To be together
Is what they need
To stop the aching
As they bleed

And when apart
They are but half
They have no joy
And cannot laugh

To hearts that beat
And live as one
Can only beat
When they are joined.

A KNIGHT TO DANCE

Upon my horse
I forge the fields
With my armor
And sword of steel

On guard I stay
It is a must
There is no one
That I will trust

I charge them all
I know no fear
I am a knight
The man of steel

The same as I
My horse of white
He's always ready
Both day and night

They cannot pierce
This armored beast
Nor touch the heart
Inside my chest

I was alert
I stayed aware
But; she bravely walked
Where no one dared

How did this lady
Who holds no lance
Capture my heart
And make it dance.

THE KEY TO MY HEART

In this old heart
There's love by the score
If you can find the key to my heart
And unlock the door

Now to my heart there's
A secret passage
But; you must first find the way
So you may unlock it

Now ever so quickly you must
Pass through a maze
And, I'm sure you must know
It will take several days;

Now making it through
Will not be a breeze,
For first you must find
All of the keys

And if you get through
Somehow, someway;
You'll find a love
That will with you
Forever stay.

HOUSE OF SILENT LOVE

Where are the sounds
That once lived in this house,
Why are my walls
As quiet as a mouse;

The silence is deadly
There is no light,
And, haunting cries I can hear
Deep in the night;

Come open my windows
Come walk through my doors
Why do I no longer
Hear footsteps upon my floor;

For so long I did sleep
Until that day
When you came along
And for me you wanted to pay;

You painted my walls
And caressed them with lumber
I was alive
No longer to slumber

Now there is no light
Not even sun
For your children no longer
Around me run;

I hear a car!
But it passes me by
And, I feel the pain in my windows
As they start to cry.

I have kept you safe
And protected you from harm,
And, I gave you shelter
Through those winter storms;

But now, you have left me here alone,
To be only a house
No longer a home.

GOD'S PALETTE

I watch the clouds
From my distant home,
They're here for a moment
And then their gone

My spirit it drifts
Beyond the stars,
Observing God's beauty
Both near and far;

With the earth he showed me
His great talent,
As he painted this canvas
With colors from his palette;

The mountain He painted
With rock and brush,
And great beauty he painted
In the desert dust;

The sunlight sparkles
From rivers and streams
And the water, it was
So pure and clean

Animals He painted
Some large, some small,
He had a purpose
For them all;

With one last touch,
He painted without word,
It was not complete
With all kinds of birds;

Then with faith and love
He placed it in the hand
Of his last creation
Known as man.

THE LAST ROSE

I write now of a flower
It may be the last we shall know,
Will this be known as our last rose?
I brought you this rose, with a smile on my face,
But, I had to watch as it withered away.

No petals are left, no beauty can it show,
Will it be known as our last rose?
From the earth it did sprout, with tiny little thorns,
And they did appear as though they were horns.

But, it grew through the night, so its beauty might show
For this little bush is known as the rose.
No petals are left, no beauty can it show,
And this will be known as our last rose.

For then came the fall, with winter on its heels,
And, now it will feel that cold winter chill.
So bury it in a box that is made of steel,
Why should it feel that cold winter chill?

You can now read these words written in stone
Here is what's left of their last rose,
No petal is left, no beauty can it show
And, now it is known as the last rose.

A BEAUTIFUL WINTER

Remember the winter
And chopping of wood,
With cool crisp morning
And how snuggling together felt so good.

The smell
As smoke boils out,
Or the sound of the kettle
With steam boiling from its spout.

The ring of an axe
While splinters do fly,
From an old peace of pine
That's already died.

Not one single tree
Showed any life,
When love sprang forth
And showed me it's light.

We meet by the creek
Where water tumbled down,
It was in the winter
Leaves covered the ground.

Remember the place
The one on the hill?
It was peace and quiet
Love gave me a chill.

Walking and talking
A hug and a kiss
You are the one I cannot resist.

YOU ASK

Your heart it beats
All through the night.
So peacefully you slept
While I held you tight.

Your skin so soft
Your body so warm
But; you didn't hold me
in your arms!

You laid on your side
Face to the well,
My back was turned
To an empty hall

Your head on my chest
I so did yearned
I heard you breathing,
Your snoring, I learned

Where was your heart beat?
This you did ask.
Well—turning you over,
That's a hell of-a-task.

Your heart beat dear
Lies in my chest.
Your back I've noticed.
"Is nothing like your breast!"

WHAT WOULD I HAVE DONE?

What would I have done?
If you'd been gone,
When I had awaken
And found, I was alone

The creaking I'd heard
Of these hollow floors
Heard each tear drop
That hit the door

Echoes of words
From last night's fight
Would say I'm dying
Deep down inside

Upon each ring of the phone
I'd pray my dreams be spared
Your voice I'd hope to hear
Saying your still cared

What would I have done
At home all alone
I'd cry and wish and pray
That you would please come home.

OUR DANCE

Dance with me lady
This I did say
I—am your knight,
Tonight; is our day!

I've searched high and low
Gone too many miles
My weapon is love
My armor a smile

The door to your heart,
This day; it is mine
It's been in my chest
All of this time

I've charged all the fields
Rivers I forged
I've fought many battles
To knock on your door

Take now my hand
This is our chance
Life; we will share
This is; our dance.

IF I COULD BE BOSS

I took a look
Out of my sleeper
I thought today;
Today will be cheerful

But I shouldn't raise
My sleepy head
I really should've
Stayed in bed

Had a blow out
And one flat tire
Got another that's
Showing wire

Had my plans worked
Out to a T,
Until the boss
Changed 'em for me

Now I don't know what to do
And I'm just as lost
As an old goose

Shreveport's where I wanted to go
But; the boss said take it to Monroe

I wish I could be
Boss for a day
Cause I'd run him
Every which way

I'd have him lost
And so confused
Until I was sure
He'd blown a fuse

Then I'd really start
Start on him.
Oops—gotta go
The boss just walked in.

I HEARD MORE

I will be your
Forever more
But—it sounded so different
When you slammed the door

My love for you
Will last and last.
But those words sure sounded
Like something in the past.

I live for you,
That's what you said
But those words came
From a heart that's dead

I will with you spend
The rest of my life
But that sound it came,
From the distant sky

Your love for me
Its burning desire
But I was consumed
By an unearthly fire

SUMMERS RETURN

Autumn approaches with
Such great speed
It soon will change
The color of leaves

Green turns yellow
Red turns brown
A carpet of gold
Will cover the ground

Birds now sing
While locust call out.
Winter approaches
They scream and shout.

Blankets of snow
Will lie around
And bring more beauty
Upon the ground

The frozen rivers
Will sparkle and shine
The fish will wait
For warmer times

Spring will call
As flowers bloom
Announcing that summer
is coming soon

DESERTS OF LOVE

Walking back down this
Timeless old road
Grown over with thorns
And full of dark holes

No beauty can be seen
By this old man
For little now covers
A once beautiful sand

I now see a river
That flowed deep with love
It no longer is freed
With kisses and hugs

The leaves of the trees
They are in the past
The sun showed no mercy
And scorched all the grass

Darken by pain
An unfaithful love
The skies are now blank
No stars' shine above

Lifeless the trees
They lay in a heap
Life from their hearts
So slowly did seep

Decades will pass
Without any sounds
The joy is all gone
No peace can be found.

THE GLASS

I raise this glass
A toast to you
Two hearts that beat
Our love was true

This glass I hold
We held that day
I meant I love you
In every way

This glass I hold
Once held champagne
Together we sipped
Our love would reign

Through all times
Both good and bad
Never again would
We be sad

But; I broke your heart
You only did what's best
For you
Your love was steady
Straight and true

No tears to shed
You or I
I was wrong
I made you cry

I'm dead I now
I must say
I let love die
You went your way.

TIMES PAST

A loving wife
With children and a home
In my times past
They are long gone

Their laughter I heard
While they ran and played
Watching out the window
They brighten my days

The house I loved
Known as our home
In my times past
That now is gone

The woman I adored
She was my wife
She gave me hope;
She gave me life

That special room
In our loving home
In my times past
They're all long gone.

MY CHILD

Nothing in the world
Could make me smile
The way I do; when
I'm with my child

He is to me
So precious you see
And nothing could ever
More me please

It is so great
And so much fun
To spend a day
With my little son

To watched him as
He rides his bike
Or to go with him
Camping at night

Without a doubt
It is going grand
When; he says, I love you, Daddy
And then takes my hand

Never would I even
Think twice
I give up for him
My very own life.

PASSIONATE WOMAN

A woman's heart it's

Such a beautiful thing;
It can make you cry;
It can make you sing

The body she has
That men do need
With a passion so strong
That men do seek;

Her breast will heave
Her nostrils may flare
She wants, she needs,
She truly cares

To hold her close,
Her words to hear
To feel her breathe
Sweet love in my ear

I feel the need
Deep in my heart,
To feel the passion
Right from the start,

Your heart beat,
Race and run,
The moment you meet,
That passionate; that
Passionate woman.

STARLIGHT

You are the star
That shines so bright
You guide my way
With your loving light

Without you girl
There is no light
Though day it be
It still seems night

Your laughter—your smile
Your sweet loving charm
I need you Barbara
In my lonely arms

Your eyes they shine
With love they glow
Your heart is true
It clearly shows

I was so lost
My heart did roam
I'm no longer scared
All fear is gone

I miss your touch
Although unknown
Your heart, my love,
It is—my home.

THE LAST HEART BEAT

I want you darling
Throughout my life
I'll be with you
Thought pain and strife

I need your heart
Your hopes and dreams
Like an old locomotive
You are my steam

By your side I'll be
On the mountain top
Valleys and all
I'll be none stop

I need your love
Both night and day
My heart's with you
Forever to stay

From our days of youth
Till old we've grown
I'll be with you
When they're all gone

By your side I'll be
In times of need
Even to our very
Last heartbeat.

NUTS ABOUT YOU

I sit here now
In this silent room
Thinking of nothing
Nothing but you

The windows hold
No joy to see
Cause it all about you—
You and me

This jacket I wear
It is snow white
So pure so clean
With lonely nights

Held back I am
I am restrained
You run through my heart
And tortured my brain

This padded room
Doc says it's fine
For my lonely—needing
Tortured mind

Why do they keep
Me in this coat
With pills they keep
Me totally doped

Doc say's I'm crazy
I am insane
Call I'll do
Call out your name

WALK IN MY SHOES

Walk in my shoes,
"if" you are able
Stand on your feet;
And try, to be stable

Look through my tears,
And see what you may
Let's see; if you can find
One cheerful day

Cry now the tears
That come from the heart
That comes from a person
Who's been torn all apart

Walk in my shoes
And judge me now
And let your true feelings
Come out somehow

Sentence me sir
If you must
But, can you know your mind
Honestly trust

THE CRIPPLE CHICKEN

That old chicken, is a mighty
Fine bird
It can do things never before
Been heard

It can take you places, that's
Never been seen

Why this old bird, is everybody's
Dream
All the pretty girls, just
Sit and cry

When they see the chicken,
Pass them by
They sit and dream, even
Fantasize

Of, how it would be, just to
Take that ride
Everyone knows this loses

Could, so easily make- em a
Star
But- for now they just
Sit and gaze
And slowly, count down
The endless days

BRUISED LOVE

I now see where your heart
Stands
It's not with me, it's with
Another man

You took my heart, and ripped the
Scar
I should not have given you my
Heart

I was to you, only a
Toy
A little play thing, they gave
You some joy

Lonely days I thought were
Gone
I thought for certain I had, found
Someone

Love I hope that be
True
Just tore a scar, maybe
Two

Back I now fall it's an endless
Hole

A chill sets in, the eyes
Turn cold

A crust now forms
Upon my heart

To try and heel, this broken
Part
From my heart my blood does
Flow
I fear it may soon drown
My soul

The doubts I had, were all
True
The love I had has now
Been bruised

There's no repair that can
Be done
All I can do, - is now
run

A WINNER I WILL BE

Now once again
I sit here in jail,
As thoughts run through my head,
Like a train on a rail.

Fake charges again
That's what I face,
As I sit in this cell,
Staring out into space.

But this time,
She'll not get away,
You can bet your ass
I'll retaliate.

Now she'll be charged,
For all of her lies,
She'll sit here in jail,
With tears in her eyes.

Then maybe she'll stop
And think twice,
Before she again,
Start with her lies.

You can bet right now,
She's having a laugh,
But of all of her troubles,
She's not seen the half.

So go ahead bitch
And have your fun,
But you can bet one thing,
This will be war,
That I, will have won.

A NEW START

Upon these wings
I will fly,
And see the luscious
Clouds go by.

Ill ride on to
My destiny.
Until my heart
It is well pleased.

I'll see the moon
And touch the stars.
Until your love
It's not as far.

I'll take your heart
In kid gloves.
And gently stroke
It like a dove.

So pure and clean,
So pure at heart.
Your love to me,
Has given me a brand new start.

James Ray Chaffin Sr.
1995

THE LAST

The words you hear
I love you
Will be the last

Dreams we shared
And held so dear
Will not be dreamed
Throughout these years

The love we made
That burned so hot
Cannot be felt
For it has stopped

A thousand times
I know is due
This is, the last
I do love you.

A HEART WITHOUT A HOME

A stone without a
Grave
Stands under a willow's
Shade

And written upon this
Stone
Here lies, a heart
That has no home

Now if you find it's
Body one day
Please bring it
By this way

Tears stream down
From the tree above
For it know this heart
Died without no love

So that it can lay
To rest
With its heart

With words
Written upon the
Stone
A heart without a home

STONE WITH NO GRAVE

A weeping willow drops
down it's limbs, to shade
the ground below
it has no heart, that we
know; but still it's sorrow shows

It weeps its' tears of sadness
Both night and day
And fall upon the stone
The stone without a grave

The words are simple
Written upon this stone
Here lies a heart,
A heart without a home

Somewhere a
Body roams this earth
That walks through life
With a constant hurt

THE PAIN UNDERNEATH

I cry for help
But no one hears
Have they to me
Turned deaf ears

A smile I do wear
Or so it may seem
While down my face
Tears go unseen

Laughter in a voice
Just like thunder
While these eyes show pain
That goes deep under

There is a twinkling
In the eyes
But it is a spark
From a raging fire

There is a calm
Before the storm
Shouldn't they now
Sound the alarm

IN NEED OF LIFE

It is the heart
That breaks and cries
Although no tears may
Stain these eyes

One drop of blood
Will seep
As this heart
Brakes in two

To stain my soul
And cloud my mind
While I stager
Through these times

A darkness settles
Upon my path
But still I struggle
Trying to grasp

A thread of hope
With shattered dreams
A lifeless rope
Or so it seems

Life I need
I beg; I plead
I need to live
I need to see

THE BRIDE

Walking that road
Here all alone
Feeling no hope, no love
Not even a home

I needed to be loved
In search of you
My loving wife
You are the one
That can return my life

A life that bloomed
With bubbling joy
With dreams once filled
This old boy

A joyous retreat
In shadows now hide
As they await
The returning bride

The tide that brings
News in a glass
Of peace for ever
And of love that will last

THE OLD HEART

There lies a yearning
Deep in my soul
It is so young
But yet, it is old

No life does it have
But still it goes on
My heart it seems
Can find no home

Nights with no love
In a bed that is cold
For a heart that is young
Has grown very old

A heart that is warm
With a wall made of steal
Keeping all out, so it may
Live, it cannot face,
another

About the Author

James Ray Chaffin Sr. a.k.a. Desperado a.k.a. The Unknown Writer was born August 20th, 1956. He had seven brothers and sisters all together and one son. His parents lived very simple lives in rural Louisiana.

James Sr. lived his entire life in Louisiana. His occupation mostly consisted of driving an 18 Wheeler. However, at times he would take a break and do carpentry or other odds and ends jobs to make money. He went from living in houses to living in tents in the woods to a camper trailer in his parent's yard.

In his last months on this earth he spent his evenings after getting in from work taking care of his ailing parents and doing the things they could no longer do. He passed away on November 26th, 2012 after complications from a stroke. He was survived by his parents, his brothers and sisters, and his son.

Made in the USA
Middletown, DE
13 June 2016